STRIPES of All Types

For my wonderful siblings,

Sally, Ann, and Lee,

and to the memory of our beloved brother, Grant

Published by
PEACHTREE PUBLISHERS
1700 Chattahoochee Avenue
Atlanta, Georgia 30318-2112
www.peachtree-online.com

Art direction by Loraine M. Joyner
Typesetting by Melanie McMahon Ives

The illustrations were created in acrylic on paper.

On the front cover and endpapers: striped skunk
On the back cover: common zebra

Manufactured in December 2012 by RR Donnelley & Sons in China
10 9 8 7 6 5 4 3 2 1
First Edition

ISBN 978-1-56145-695-6 / 1-56145-695-0

Cataloging-in-Publication Data is available from the Library of Congress.

Stripes of All Types

Written and Illustrated by
Susan Stockdale

PEACHTREE
ATLANTA

Stripes found in water,

sliding through weeds.

Drinking from rivers,

and darting through reeds.

Toting a shell,

twisting on sand.

Sprawled in a lair,

and sprinting on land.

Prowling the prairie,

perched on a peak.

Crawling on cactus,

and camped by a creek.

Propped on a log,

poised on a leaf.

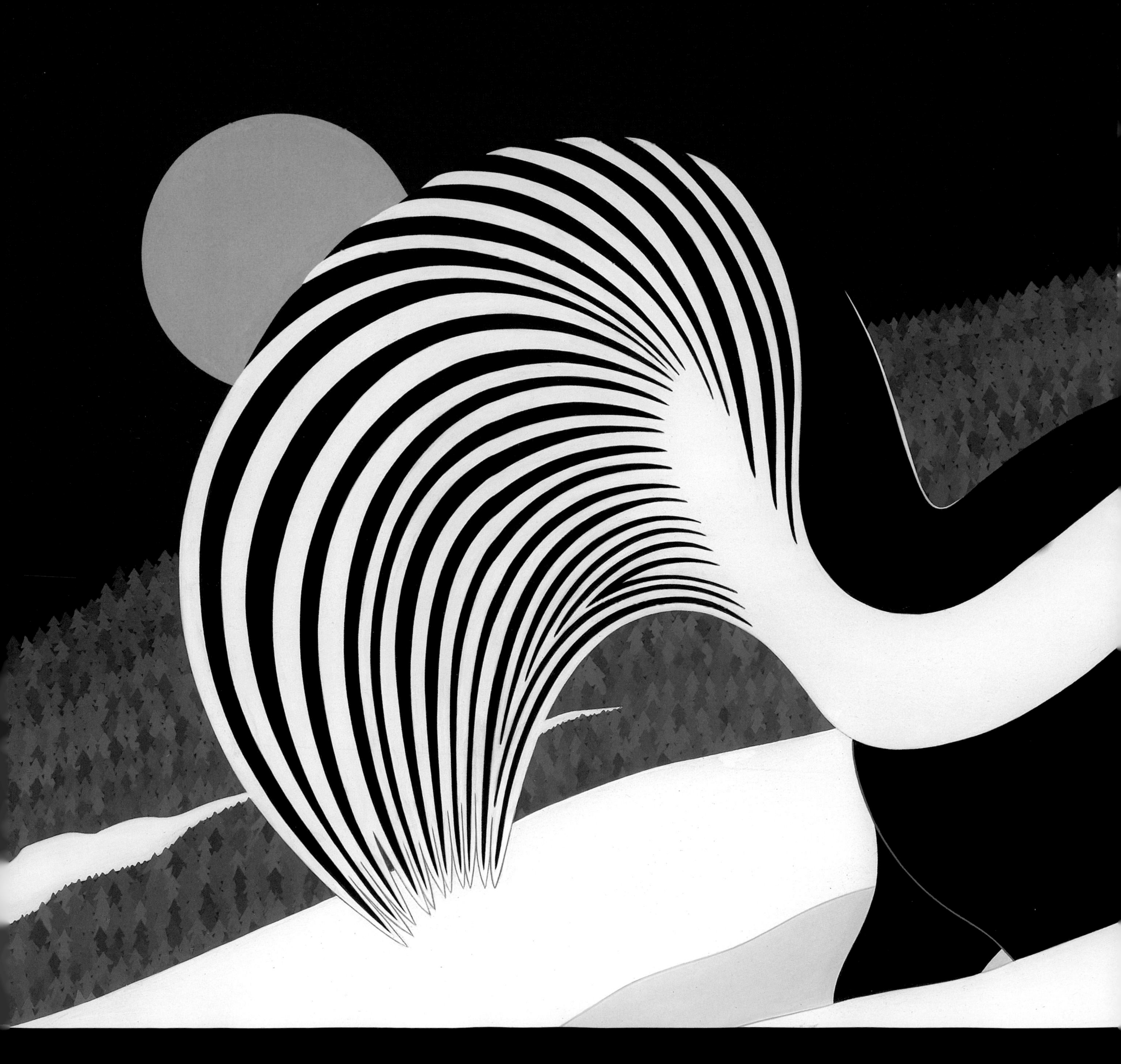

Scaling a ridge,

and scouting a reef.

Stripes found in forests,

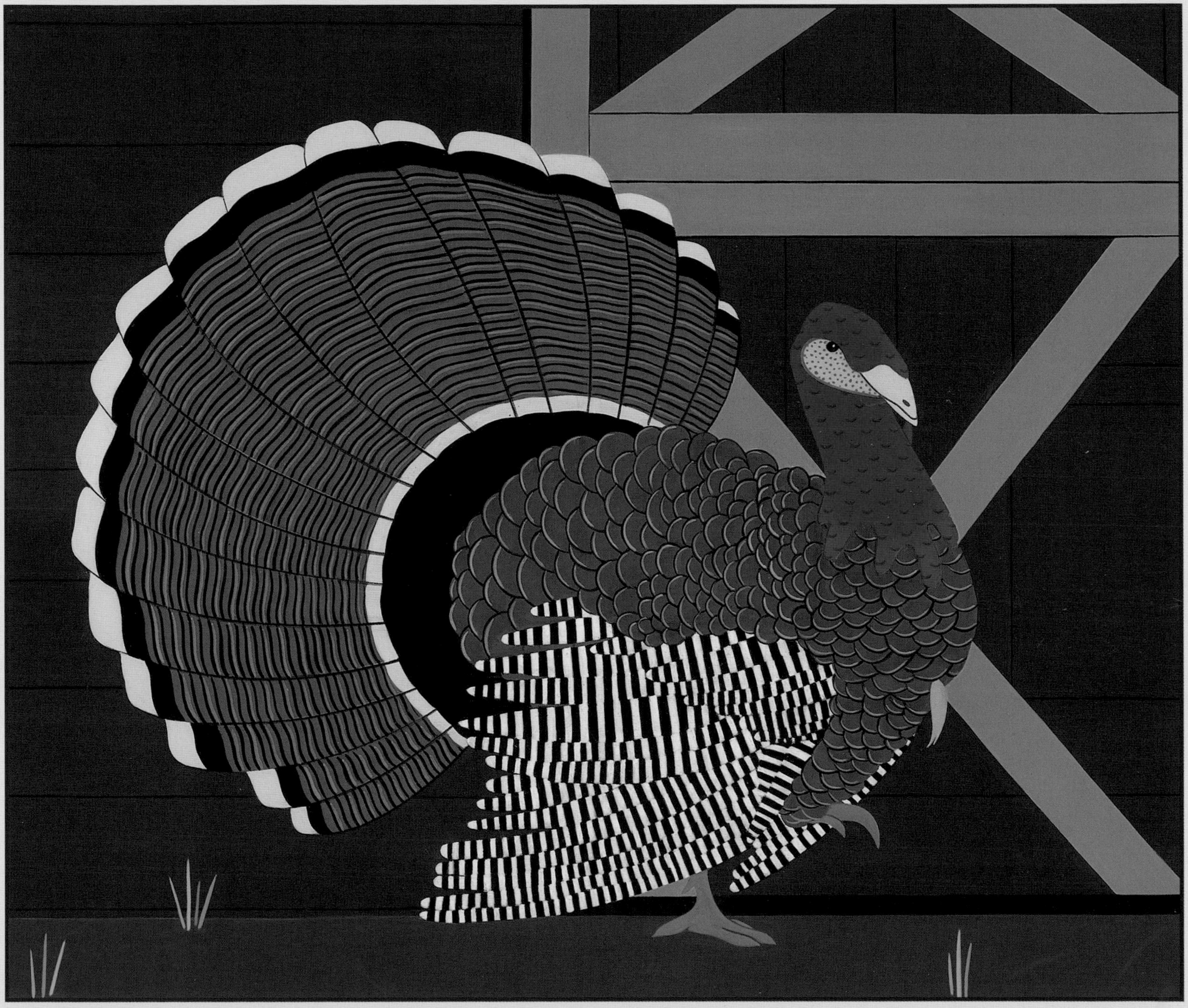

stripes found on farms.

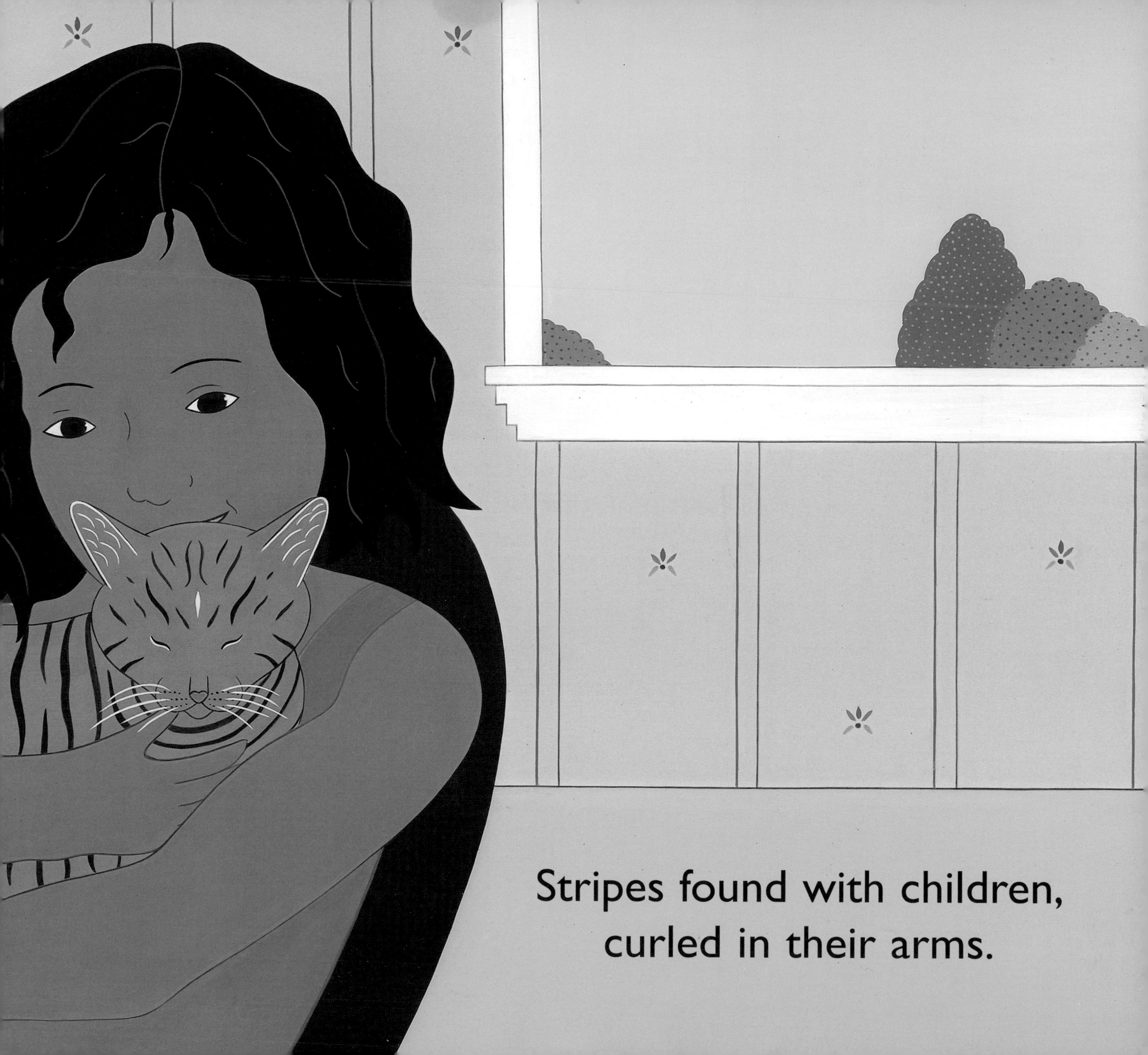

Stripes found with children,
curled in their arms.

Stinging tentacles on the adult **purple-striped jellyfish** can kill or paralyze prey. Its brightly colored stripes may alert predators to stay away. (California coast of the Pacific Ocean; invertebrate)

The striped pattern on the **eastern garter snake** helps it go unseen while it slithers along the grassy ground. (North America; reptile)

The **ring-tailed lemur** uses its distinctive black-and-white striped tail to communicate, sometimes raising it like a flag to keep group members together. (Madagascar, off the coast of Africa; mammal)

Striped feathers on the **American bittern** help camouflage it among the dense reed beds in which it lives. Though its call is booming, the bird prefers to stay hidden. (North and Central America; bird)

The **Florida tree snail** lives on smooth-barked hardwood trees and feeds on the fungi and algae that grow there. The reason for its swirling stripes is unknown. (Southeastern United States; mollusk)

Stripes on the **zebra moray eel** may help it blend with its surroundings and recognize other eels of its own kind. Its stripes increase in number as it grows larger. (Indo-Pacific Ocean and Red Sea; fish)

The **tiger**, the largest wildcat in the world, has stripes that allow it to hide among tall grasses as it stalks its prey. (South and Southeast Asia, China, and the Russian Far East; mammal)

Black and white stripes on the **common zebra** make it hard for predators to distinguish a single animal from the herd. No two zebras' stripes are exactly alike. (Africa; mammal)

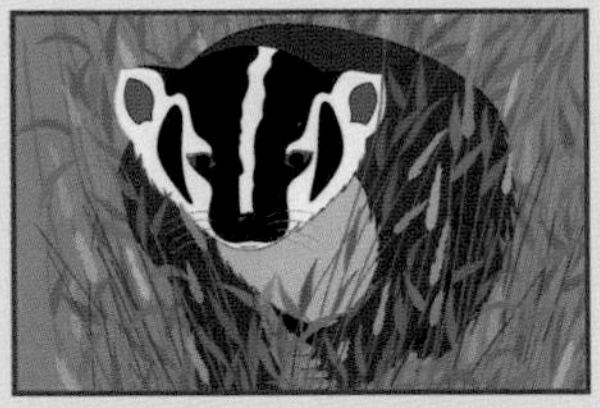

Two black stripes help conceal the eyes of the **American badger**, making it less visible to its enemies as it hunts for food in the tall prairie grass. (North America; mammal)

Vertical white stripes on the **bongo** break up its body outline so that it blends with its wooded surroundings. (Africa; mammal)

The black and yellow stripes on the **cactus bee** may serve as a warning to predators. If threatened, the bee will defend itself by injecting venom from its stinger. (North and South America; arthropod)

A baby **Malayan tapir** has stripes to help it hide in the forest. As the tapir grows up, the stripes fade away. (Southeast Asia; mammal)

Bright stripes on the **phantasmal poison frog** are a signal to potential predators that it is toxic. Scientists have used the poison produced by this frog to help develop effective painkillers for humans. (South America; amphibian)

Stripes on the wings of the **zebra swallowtail butterfly** create visual confusion for predators, so they don't know which part of the butterfly's body to attack. (North America; arthropod)

The **striped skunk** has bold stripes that warn other animals to stay away. When a skunk is threatened, it produces an oily, smelly spray that repels most predators. (North America; mammal)

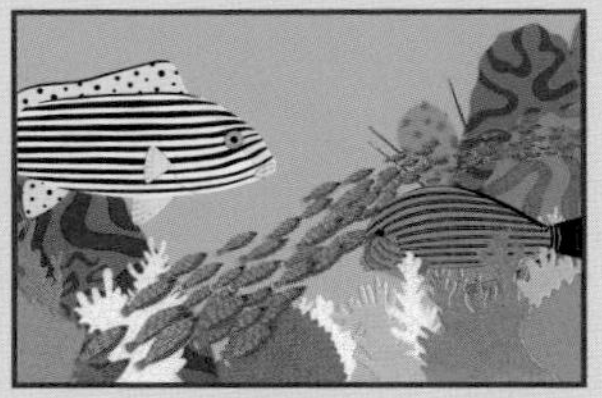

Many fishes, such as the **striped surgeonfish**, **sixline wrasse**, and **oriental sweetlips**, have colorful stripes that identify them to other fishes of their own kind and may also help camouflage them among the coral reefs. (Indo-Pacific Ocean; fish)

White, horizontal stripes on the legs of the **okapi** help it hide from predators in the dense jungle. This rare forest giraffe is a fast runner and a good jumper. (Africa; mammal)

To attract a female, the male **turkey** displays his striped, fan-shaped tail feathers and produces a distinctive gobble that can be heard a mile away. (North America; bird)

The **mackerel tabby** and some other domestic cats retain the striped pattern of the African wildcat, their direct ancestor. (worldwide; mammal)

Can you find the animals that belong to these STRIPES?

ring-tailed lemur

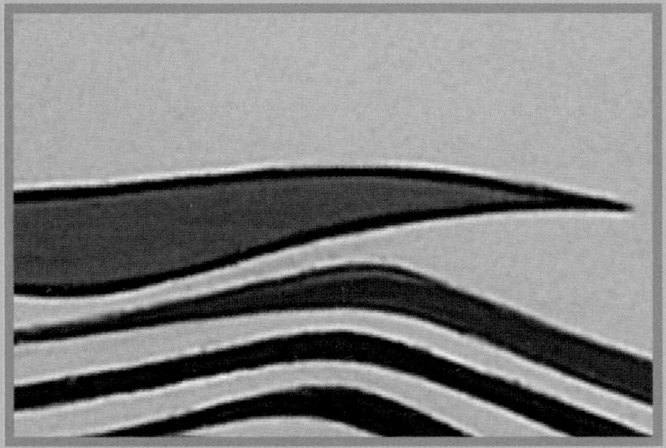

American bittern

cactus bee

bongo

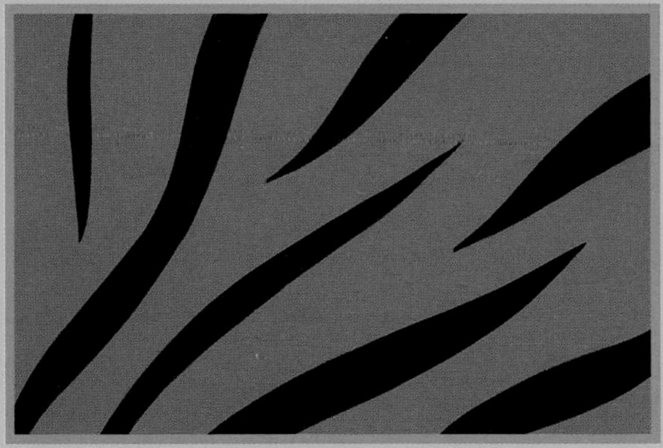

tiger

Florida tree snail

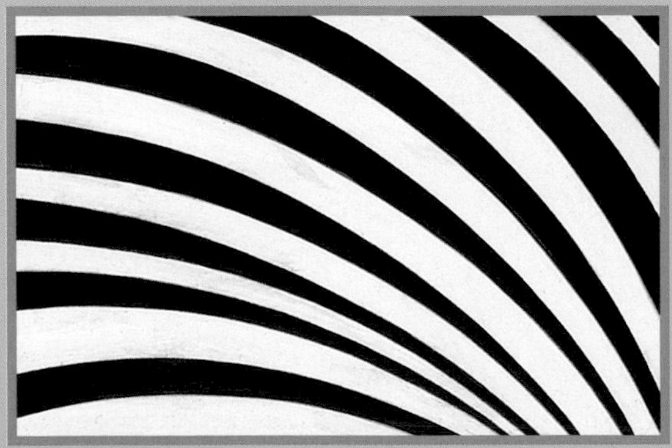

striped skunk

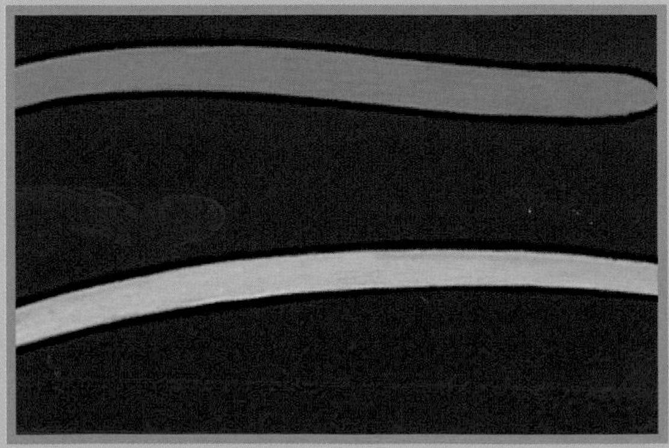

phantasmal poison frog

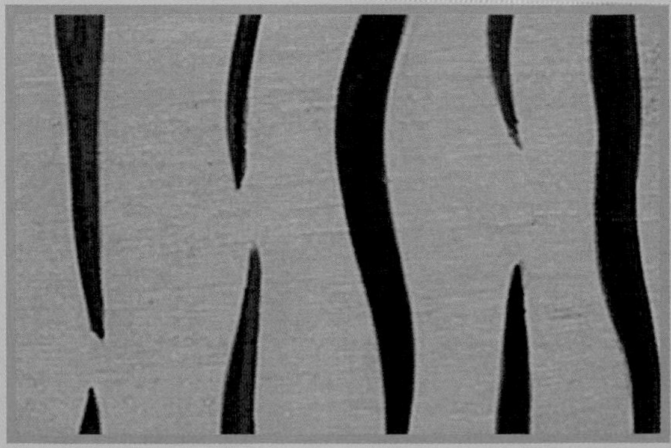

mackerel tabby

turkey

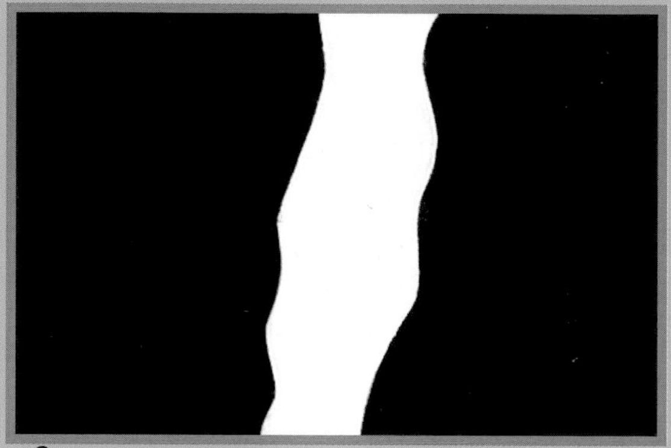
American badger

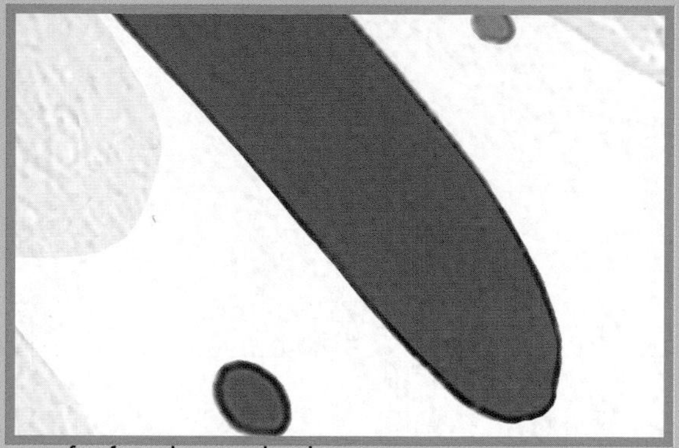
purple-striped jellyfish

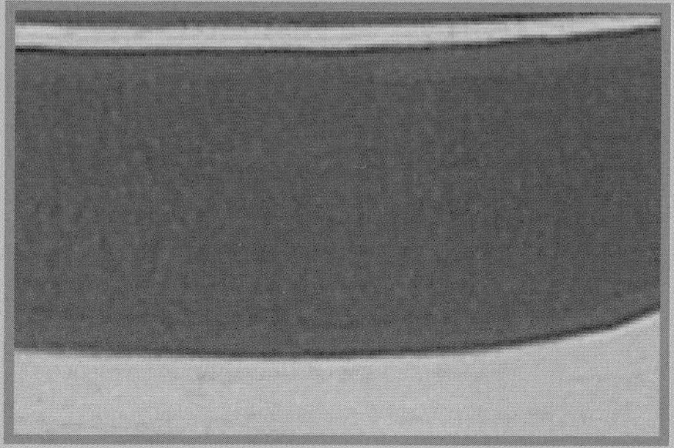
eastern garter snake

okapi

zebra swallowtail butterfly

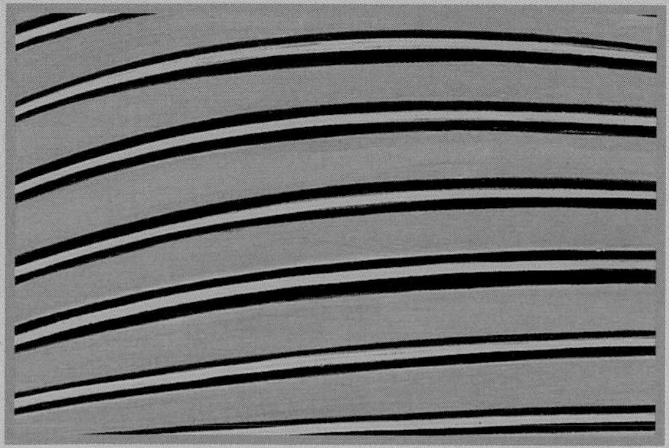
striped surgeonfish

common zebra

zebra moray eel

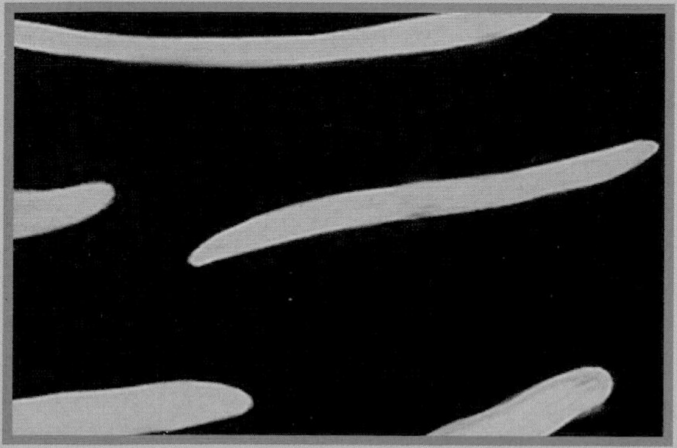
Malayan tapir

Turn the book upside down
to read the correct answers.

I am grateful to many scientists at the Smithsonian Institution's National Museum of Natural History for their valuable research assistance. They include Dr. Allen Collins, Dr. Kevin de Queiroz, Dr. Carla Dove, Dr. Jerry Harasewych, Mr. Gary F. Hevel, Dr. Dave Johnson, and Dr. Victor G. Springer.

I am especially thankful to Dr. Kristofer Helgen, also of the National Museum of Natural History, for his help regarding the many mammals in this book.